The FJH Recorder Method for Everyone

FREE Downloadable Recordings!

Andrew Balent
Philip Groeber

CONTENTS

Production: Frank Hackinson
Production Coordinator: Philip Groeber
Cover Design: Terpstra Design, San Francisco
Interior Drawings: Nina Crittenden and Andi Whitmer
Engraving: Tempo Music Press, Inc.

Printer: Tempo Music Press, Inc.
Recorded by: Sharon Howell (recorder),
    Joe Wehunt (piano)
Recording Engineer: Joe Wehunt
Recorder Consultants: Rebecca Gerhardt and Sharen Hafner

THE FJH MUSIC COMPANY INC.
Frank J. Hackinson

ISBN-13: 978-1-61928-050-2

MW01110345

GETTING STARTED

Assemble your recorder

Recorders can come in one, two, or three parts. Assemble the recorder using the diagram on the right. Be sure to line up the holes as shown. The soprano recorder is one of the smallest recorders and plays very high notes.

Posture

Keep your back straight whether sitting or standing. Your back as well as your shoulders, arms, hands, and fingers all need to be relaxed. Avoid any tension as it can affect your tone, breath, and the muscle movements in your hands and fingers.

Hand and finger position

Left Hand Your left hand is placed at the top of the recorder, closest to your mouth. Place your thumb over the hole on the back of the recorder. Your first three fingers cover the holes 1, 2, and 3.

Right Hand Your right hand is placed at the bottom of the recorder. Your thumb is placed on the back of the recorder for balance. Your four fingers cover the holes 4, 5, 6, and 7. Rotate the foot joint so that your little finger rests comfortably on the 7th hole.

Curve all of your fingers slightly and completely cover the holes with the fleshy part of your fingertips.

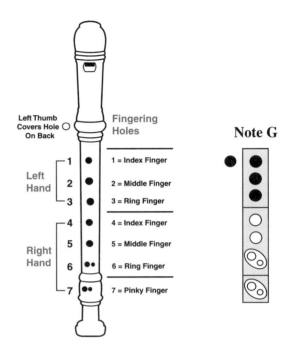

Embouchure

Place the mouthpiece of the recorder on your bottom lip and in front of the bottom teeth. Do not close your top teeth down on the mouthpiece. Press down very gently with your upper lip by whispering "mmm". This will put your mouth in the correct position. Be careful not to let your tongue or your teeth touch the mouthpiece. Make sure that your lips stay firm around the mouthpiece. Don't open and close your mouth on each note. This will help to avoid air leaks.

Getting a good tone

Blow with a steady, gentle and warm air stream, not too hard. Play your first note B (see page 4). Blow gently, starting the air by saying "tu." Be sure the holes are completely covered.

If you blow too hard there will be a squeaking noise.

Cleaning your recorder

After playing, dry the inside of your recorder with a cotton swab or lint-free cloth. Keep the mouthpiece clean.

Introduction

I-1052

MUSIC FUNDAMENTALS

THE TREBLE CLEF

The **treble** (or **G**) **clef** is placed at the beginning (left side) of each staff of recorder music.

THE STAFF

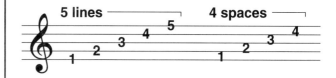

Music is written on the **staff**, which has five lines and four spaces.

LINE NOTES

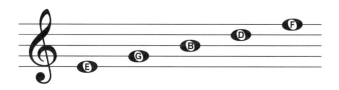

Each **line** has a letter name:

Every **G**ood **B**oy **D**oes **F**ine

SPACE NOTES

Each **space** has a letter name:

F A C E

PITCH

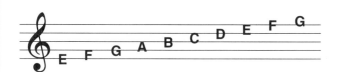

Pitch is the highness or lowness of a music tone. The higher the pitch, the higher a note is placed on the staff. The lower the pitch, the lower a note is placed on the staff. The names of notes come from the music alphabet A–G.

NOTE AND REST VALUES

o	—	**whole**	= 4 beats
d.		**dotted half**	= 3 beats
d	—	**half**	= 2 beats
♩	𝄽	**quarter**	= 1 beat
♪	𝄾	**eighth**	= ½ beat

Note values (o d. d ♩ ♪) indicate the duration of each pitch. Each musical note indicates the pitch to be played *and* how long to let the tone sound. A rest is a period of silence.

BAR LINES AND MEASURES

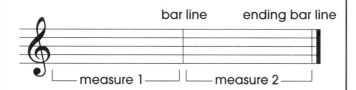

Bar lines divide the staff into equal parts called **measures**. An **ending bar line** is used to show the end of a piece of music.

THE TIME SIGNATURE

The $\frac{4}{4}$ (four-four) **time signature** tells us:

4 = four beats per measure
4 = the quarter note (♩) gets one beat

Count: 1   2   3   4

NEW NOTES B AND A

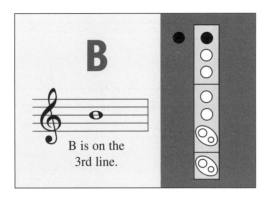

B is on the 3rd line.

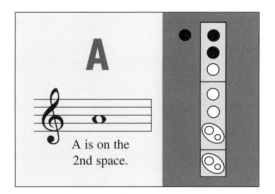

A is on the 2nd space.

NOTES AND RESTS

The **whole note** and **whole rest** get four beats. o = 4 beats   ▬ = 4 beats

The **quarter note** and the **quarter rest** get one beat.   ♩ = 1 beat   𝄽 = 1 beat

A rest is a period of silence.

Always keep an even, steady beat.

New Note Studies (Remember, "Left hand on top!")

Student Duet (Play Part 1, then play Part 2)

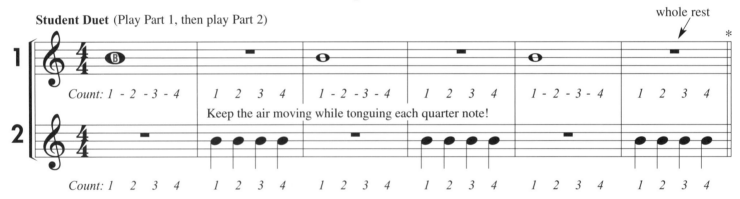

Lines 1 and 2 can be played together as a *duet* (two different parts played together).

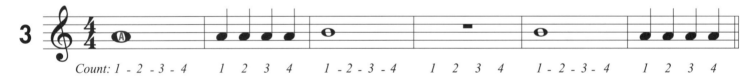

Be sure you are not making a sound during a rest. A rest is a good time to take a breath.

Smooth Sailing

②

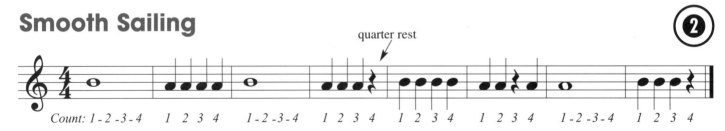

recorder tip *The recorder has a very pretty and clear musical sound called its* **tone**. *To create this clear tone, relax your neck and facial muscles, inhale, and softly say the syllable "tu" as you gently blow the air into the mouthpiece. This technique is referred to as your* **articulation**.

* Two thin bar lines indicate the end of an exercise or the end of a section of a song.

I-1052

Rock It!

5 ← measure number

MUSICAL TERMS

Music uses many terms, some are in English, many are Italian. Here are a few of the basic terms.

melody the succession of pitches in a song

rhythm the movement of notes in time

legato playing the melody in a smooth, connected manner

tempo indicates the speed of the music

Andante a slow tempo

Moderato a medium tempo

Allegro a fast tempo

Here are several "big picture" tips that will help you learn to play the recorder quickly and have a lot of fun while doing it.

1) The more you practice, the easier it becomes, the faster you learn.

2) You are learning a new language, the language of music. The beginning stages are very important. You want to learn as much as you can so you are able to read and communicate this new language with others.

3) You can also play music written for any instrument that uses the treble (G) clef such as the flute, trumpet, clarinet, saxophone, and violin.

4) Play with other musicians as often as you can: classmates, family and relatives, neighborhood friends, etc.

NEW NOTE G

G is on the 2nd line.

New Note Study

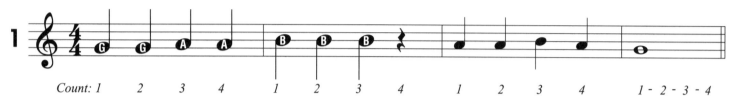

1

Count: 1 2 3 4   1 2 3 4   1 2 3 4   1 - 2 - 3 - 4

HALF NOTES AND RESTS

 or

The **half note** and the **half rest** get two beats. ♩ = 2 beats   ▬ = 2 beats

Be sure to let the half note sound for two full beats.

Half Note Studies

half rest

2

Count: 1 - 2 3 - 4   1 - 2 3 - 4   1 - 2 3 - 4   1 - 2 3 4   1 2 3 4   1 2 3 - 4

Allegro

3

Count: 1 - 2 3 - 4   1 2 3 - 4   1 - 2 3 4   1 2 3 - 4   1 2 3 - 4   1 2 3 - 4

4

Count: 1 - 2 3 - 4   1 2 3 - 4   1 - 2 3 4   1 2 3 4   1 2 3 - 4   1 2 3 - 4   1 2 3 - 4   1 2 3 - 4

Hot Cross Buns

English Folksong

Today, *Hot Cross Buns* is a popular children's song, but originally it was sung by street vendors in England to encourage customers to buy their bread and other food items.

Moderato

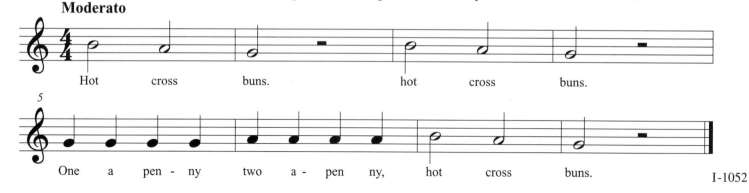

Hot   cross   buns.   hot   cross   buns.

5

One   a   pen-ny   two   a-pen-ny,   hot   cross   buns.

6

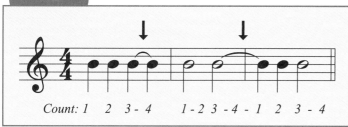

A **tie** connects two notes that are on the same line or space. Tongue the *first note only*, allowing it to sound for the combined value of both notes.

Rhythm Study

5

Always support your breath. Be sure to breathe from the diaphragm and blow evenly. This will keep your sound consistent.

BREATH MARK

A **breath mark** is a comma symbol that tells you when to take a breath. The previous note will therefore be a little shorter in duration, but the tempo will not be affected. Remember, a rest is a good time to take a breath!

(5)

Au Clair de la lune

French Folksong

take a breath

Andante

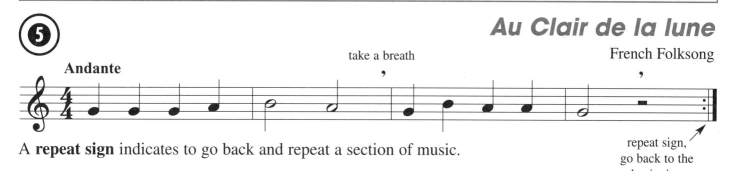

A **repeat sign** indicates to go back and repeat a section of music.

repeat sign, go back to the beginning

(6)

Merrily We Roll Along

Traditional

Allegro

Mer - ri - ly we roll a - long, roll a - long, roll a - long.

5

Mer - ri - ly we roll a - long. o'er the deep blue sea.

Pay close attention to your articulation and tone. Be sure to get a clear, pretty sound. Carefully connecting the notes to each other (legato) along with getting a good tone will make your recorder sing!

NEW NOTES D AND E

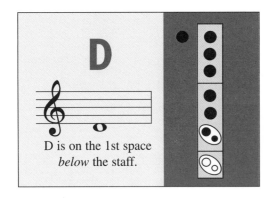
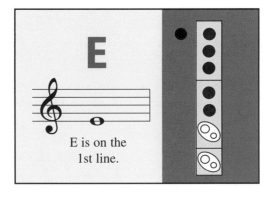

The new notes D and E are the first notes you have learned that require using the right hand.

New Note Study

 Blow a little softer for the note D to help get a good sound. Be sure that your third finger covers both holes.

Let's Keep Movin' ⑦

Tricky Fingers ⑧

In *Tricky Fingers*, repeat from the very beginning.

 **Check this out, the recorder and its presence in popular music!**
The Beatles, *The Fool on the Hill*   The Rolling Stones, *Ruby Tuesday*
Led Zeppelin, *Stairway to Heaven*   Yes, *The Yes Album*

Jolly Old Saint Nicholas

Traditional

Allegro

Jol - ly Old Saint Nich - o - las, lean your ear this way!

Don't you tell a sin - gle soul, what I'm going to say.

Christ - mas Eve is com - ing soon, now you dear old man;

Whis - per what you'll bring to me, tell me if you can.

Down to the Beach

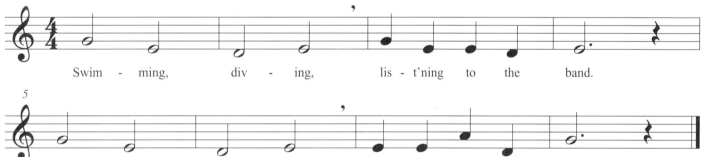

Swim - ming, div - ing, lis - t'ning to the band.

Boog - ie board - ing, glid - ing on the sand.

Mixing It Up!

Moderato

music master

Circle the measures that contain an incorrect number of beats.
Look at the top number of the time signature to help you.
Does the music sound familiar?

NEW NOTE F♯

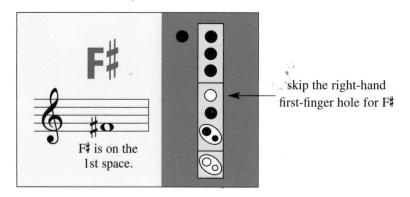

skip the right-hand
first-finger hole for F♯

F♯ is on the
1st space.

A **sharp** (♯) *raises* the pitch of a note by a **half step**.
The sharp symbol stays in effect until the end of a measure.

New Note Study

F is still played
as a sharp

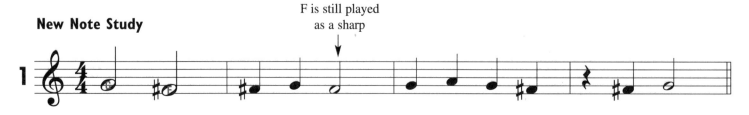

THE KEY OF G MAJOR

When notes of a song are centered around the note G, the song is said to be in the **key of G major**. When this occurs, all of the F notes in the song need to be played as a sharp. The **key signature** will remind you what note to play sharp. Notice the sharp symbol that is placed on the F line of the staff. This indicates that all F notes are going to be played as sharps, even though this is not indicated before each note.

Mary, Mary Will You Marry Me?

American Folksong

key signature   The arrows indicate which notes are to be played sharp as indicated by the key signature.

Hey, Betty Martin

American Folksong

Tip: Always look for the key signature before starting a song.

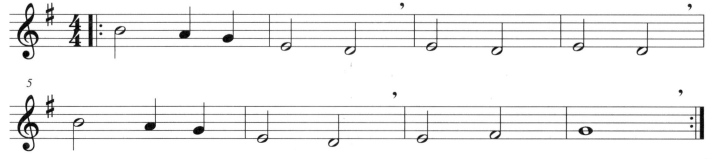

I-1052

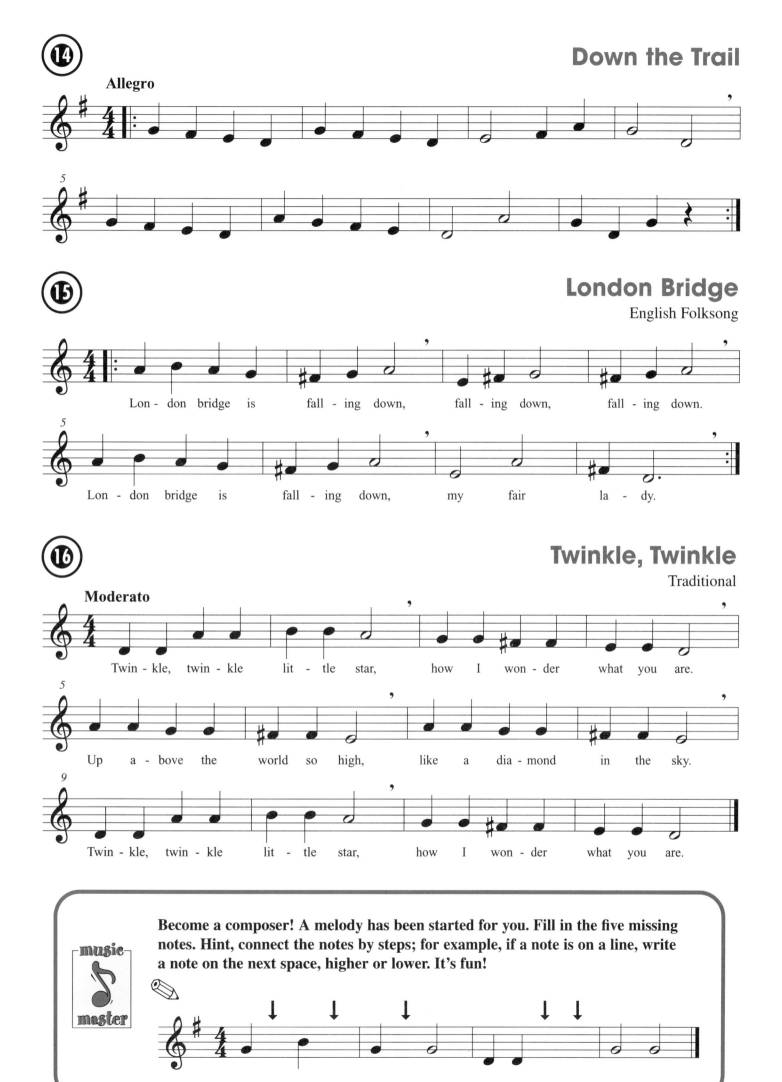

3/4 TIME SIGNATURE

Music with a **3/4 time signature** gets three beats per measure.
Each beat is equal to one quarter note.

DOTTED HALF NOTES

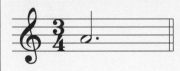

Count: 1 - 2 - 3

A dot placed after a note increases the value of the note by
one half of its value. The **dotted half note** gets *three* beats.

♩ (2 beats) + ♩ (1 beat) = ♩. (3 beats)

Rhythm Study in 3/4 Time *(Be sure you are counting three beats in a measure!)*

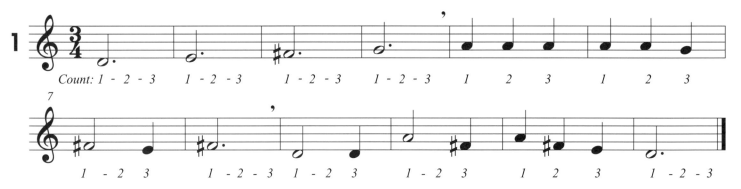

Move Those Fingers

Oh, Dear! What Can the Matter Be?

English Folksong

Moderato

The recorder achieved it's greatest popularity in the
renaissance era (ca. 1430–1650). King Henry the VIII
(1491–1547) of England is said to have owned over
75 recorders!

PICK-UP NOTES

Count: (1 2 3) 4   1   2   3   4   1   2   3

Pick-up notes are notes that come before the first complete measure. The beats in the pick-up measure and the last measure usually add up to one complete measure.

⑲

For He's A Jolly Good Fellow
Traditional English Melody

Count: (1 2) 3   1 - 2   3

🖝 = *fermata*, hold the note longer than usual

⑳

Michael, Row the Boat Ashore
African-American Spiritual

1st and 2nd endings - Play the first ending only and then take the repeat.
Then play the second ending, only, skipping over the first ending.

 **music master** Playing in an ensemble can also allow someone to be a soloist.
In *Michael, Row the Boat Ashore*, pick one or more members of your ensemble to play the part marked SOLO. The rest of the ensemble plays the part marked ALL. Take turns being the soloist.

NEW NOTE C

C is on the
3rd space.

New Note Study

1

2

Write in the note names.

Barcarolle 〈21〉

Jacques Offenbach (1819–1880)

A *barcarolle* is a boat song sung by the gondoliers in Venice, Italy.
The theme of *Barcarolle* is taken from the opera *The Tales of Hoffman,* premiered in 1851.

Moderato

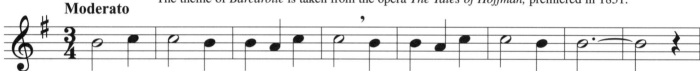

Aura Lee 〈22〉

Traditional Folksong

Andante

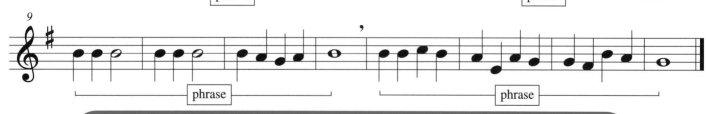

A phrase is a succession of notes which make up a musical idea.
The use of the breath mark in recorder music indicates where
these musical thoughts begin and end.

14

I-1052

The Snake Charmer
Traditional

Andante

Yankee Doodle
American Folksong

Allegro

Bingo
Traditional Children's Song

Allegro

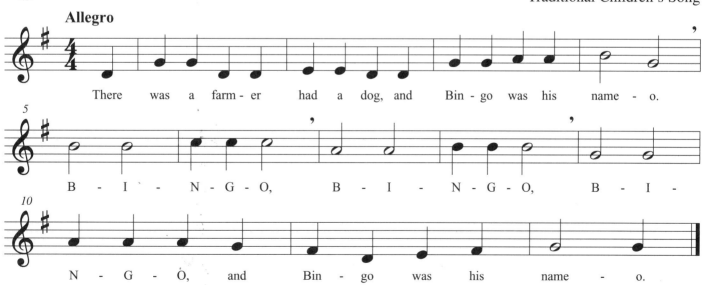

There was a farm-er had a dog, and Bin-go was his name - o.

B - I - N-G-O, B - I - N - G-O, B - I -

N - G - O, and Bin - go was his name - o.

This book includes several songs from different parts of the world. Some songs are famous themes, and others are about a particular dance or children's game. If there is a song that reminds you of your nationality, research the song to find out more about it.

EIGHTH NOTES

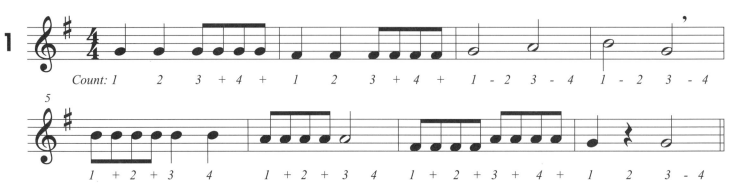

A quarter note can be divided into two equal parts called **eighth notes**. A single eighth note has a **flag** (♪). Two or more eighth notes may be connected by a **beam** (♫).

♪ = ½ beat   ♫ = 1 beat   ♫♫ = 2 beats

Be sure you play eighth notes very smoothly and evenly.
Count: 1 + (and) 2 + 3 + 4 + as you play.

Rhythm Study

1

Count: 1   2   3 + 4 +   1   2   3 + 4 +   1 - 2   3 - 4   1 - 2   3 - 4

5

1 + 2 + 3   4   1 + 2 + 3   4   1 + 2 + 3 + 4 +   1   2   3 - 4

Duet A duet is a piece of music for two performers. The ability to play well with others is one of the top requirements of a good musician. Learn to play both Parts I and II of each duet.

Waltzing Recorders

(26)

Student Duet

melody

harmony

Switch parts on the repeat.

Going to Kentucky

(27)

American Folksong

Moderato

I-1052

Hush Little Baby

Traditional

Andante

1. Hush, lit - tle ba - by, don't say a word,
2. If that___ dia - mond ring turns___ brass,

Pa - pa's gon - na buy you a mock - ing - bird.
Pa - pa's gon - na buy you a look - ing glass.

If that mock - ing - bird won't sing,
If that look - ing glass gets broke,

Pa - pa's gon - na buy you a dia - mond ring.
Pa - pa's gon - na buy you a bil - ly goat.

This Old Man

Traditional Children's Song

Andante

1. This old man, he played one;
2. This old man, he played two;

He played knick - knack on my thumb. With a
He played knick - knack on my shoe. With a

knick - knack, pad - dy whack, give the dog a bone;

This old man came roll - ing home.

The recorder has a whistle mouthpiece built into the instrument itself, which is different from other wind instruments as the flute, clarinet, and saxophone. Your air stream automatically produces a tone, whereas other wind instrumentalists need to learn to control their lip muscles. This mouthpiece, at the end of the recorder's tube, is called the **fipple**.

NEW NOTE F

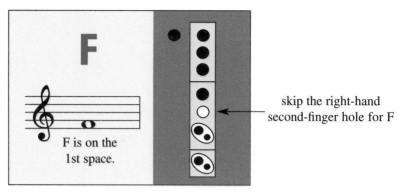

F is on the
1st space.

skip the right-hand
second-finger hole for F

Be sure that your third and fourth fingers of your right hand
cover both of the holes. Move your fingers at the same time.

New Note Study

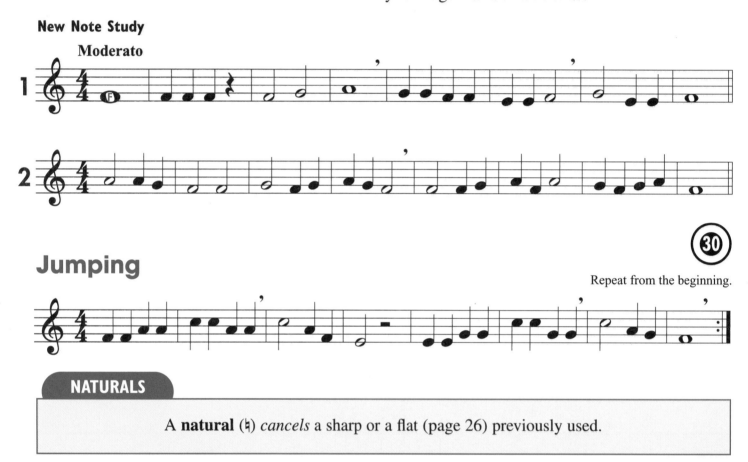

Jumping

Repeat from the beginning.

NATURALS

A **natural** (♮) *cancels* a sharp or a flat (page 26) previously used.

Time to Be Natural

recorder tip *Remember that proper articulation, breath support, and posture are necessary to produce a beautiful tone on your recorder. Listen to yourself and compare your tone to others in your ensemble.*

I-1052

White Coral Bells

Traditional Round

Allegro

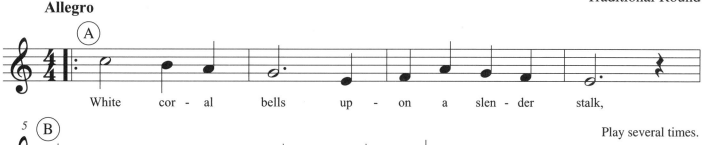

White cor - al bells up - on a slen - der stalk,

Play several times.

li - lies of the val - ley dress my gar - den walk.

> **music master**
>
> A round is a song in which the music can be repeated over and over, with the performers starting and ending at different times. In *White Coral Bells*, the first group starts at letter A. The second group starts at the beginning when the first group gets to letter B.

My Hat, It Has Three Corners

German Folksong

Moderato

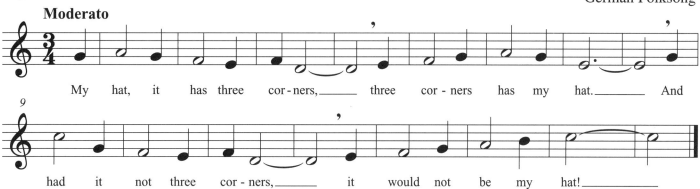

My hat, it has three cor - ners,_____ three cor - ners has my hat._____ And

had it not three cor - ners,_____ it would not be my hat!_____

CONDUCTING

Conducting is a wonderful experience for young musicians. If your teacher asks you to conduct your group, give it a try!

Here are some tips. 1) Know the music well.
2) Place your right hand in a handshake position and practice the conducting gestures below often, until you can do them without thinking about it.
3) Make eye contact with everyone before starting.
4) Count out the tempo before you start.
In 4/4 time give one measure, in 3/4 and 2/4 time give two measures.
5) Make your gestures as clear and precise as you can, especially to create a solid ending.

4/4 time

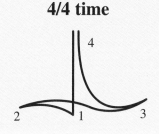

3/4 time

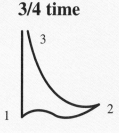

2/4 time

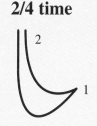

NEW NOTE HIGH D

High D is on
the 4th line.

To help balance the recorder while playing High D, press your right-hand thumb up
while pressing your left-hand middle finger down.

New Note Studies

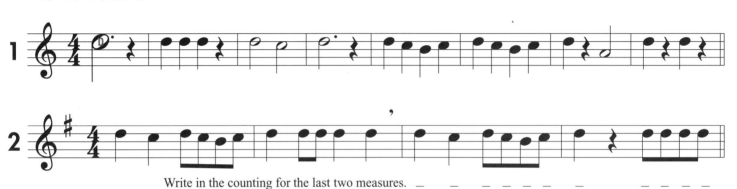

Write in the counting for the last two measures.

Sur le pont d'Avignon
On the Bridge at Avignon

French Folksong

D.C. al Fine means go back to the very beginning of the song and end at the word *Fine*.

The word *Fine* (FEE-nay) indicates the end of the piece.

Check this out, the recorder and its presence in popular music!
Jimmy Buffett, *Changes in Latitudes, Changes in Attitudes*
Mannheim Steamroller, various albums
Fairport Convention, various albums   Billy Joel, *Rosalinda's Eyes*
Keith Jarrett, *Spirits*   Bruce Springsteen, various albums

I-1052

NEW NOTE LOW C

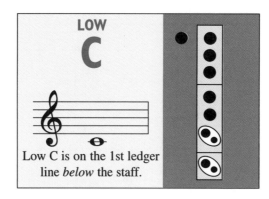

LOW
C

Low C is on the 1st ledger line *below* the staff.

This is the lowest note on the recorder. Be sure that all of the holes are covered.
Blow gently and articulate softly to get a good tone. Think LOW!

New Note Study

1

Down We Go!

Andante

Skipping

Moderato

On Top of Old Smokey

American Folksong

Moderato

On top of Old Smok - ey,_____ all cov-ered with snow,_____ I

lost my true lov - er,_____ for court - in' too slow._____

THE KEY OF C MAJOR

When notes of a song are centered around the note C, the song is said to be in the **key of C major**. Below are the notes that comprise the C major scale. Memorize this scale and practice it often, ascending and descending.

smoothly

Musette
Johann Sebastian Bach (1685–1750)

Andante

Lavender's Blue
English Folksong

Moderato

Pop! Goes the Weasel
English Folksong

Allegro

All a - round the mul - ber - ry bush, the mon - key

chased the wea - sel. The mon - key thought 'twas

all___ in fun. Pop! Goes the wea - sel.

DOTTED QUARTER NOTES

The **dotted quarter note** gets one and one half beats. ♩. = 1½ beats
The note following a dotted quarter note will often be an eighth note (♪).

Rhythm Studies

1

Count: 1 - 2 + 3   4   1 - 2 + 3   4   1 - 2 + 3   4   1 - 2 - 3   4

2

Count: 1 - 2 + 3   4   1 - 2 + 3   4   1 - 2 + 3   4   1 - 2 - 3   4

Lines 1 and 2 should sound the same.

Jingle Bells

James Pierpont (1822–1893)

Jin - gle bells,   jin - gle bells,   jin - gle all   the   way.   Oh, what fun it

is   to ride in a   one - horse o - pen   sleigh._____   one - horse o - pen   sleigh.

Ode to Joy
Theme from the Ninth Symphony

Ludwig van Beethoven (1770–1827)

I-1052

All Through the Night

Welsh Folksong

Count: 1 - 2 + 3   4   1 - 2 + 3   4   1 - 2 3 4 +   1 - 2 - 3 - 4

Goodnight Ladies

Traditional

Good - night   la - dies,   fare - well   gen - tle - men.   Sweet   dreams   ev - 'ry - one,   we're

go - ing   to   leave   you   now.   Mer - ri - ly   we   roll   a - long,   roll   a - long,

roll   a - long.   Mer - ri - ly   we   roll   a - long,   o - ver   the   deep   blue   sea.

Saint Anthony's Chorale

Franz Joseph Haydn (1732–1809)

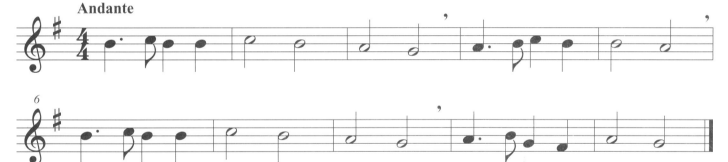

Amazing Grace

Traditional American Melody

NEW NOTE B♭

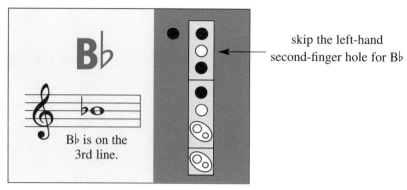

skip the left-hand
second-finger hole for B♭

A **flat** (♭) *lowers* the pitch of a note by a **half step**.
The flat symbol stays in effect until the end of a measure.

New Note Studies — B is still played as a flat

Frère Jacques
Are You Sleeping?

Traditional French Children's Round (4 part)

Frè - re Jac - ques, frè - re Jac - ques, dor - mez - vous? Dor - mez - vous?
Are you sleep - ing? Are you sleep ing? Broth - er John, Broth er John.

Son - nez les ma - ti - nes! Son - nez les ma - ti - nes! Din, dan, don! Din, dan, don!
Morn-ing bells are ring-ing! Morn-ing bells are ring-ing! Ding, dong, ding! Ding, dong, ding!

America

Words by Samuel F. Smith (1808–1895) Music: *Thesaurus Musicus* (1744)

My coun - try, 'tis of thee, sweet land of lib - er - ty,

of thee I sing; Land where my fa - thers died, land of the

pil - grims' pride, from ev 'ry___ moun - tain side let___ free - dom ring.

I-1052

THE KEY OF F MAJOR

When notes of a song are centered around the note F, the song is said to be in the **key of F major**. When this occurs, all of the B notes in the song need to be played as a flat. The **key signature** will remind you what note to play flat. Notice the flat symbol that is placed on the B line of the staff. This indicates that all B notes are going to be played as flats, even though this is not indicated before each note.

Arrorró mi niño
Argentinian Folksong

The arrows indicate which notes are to be played flat as indicated by the key signature.

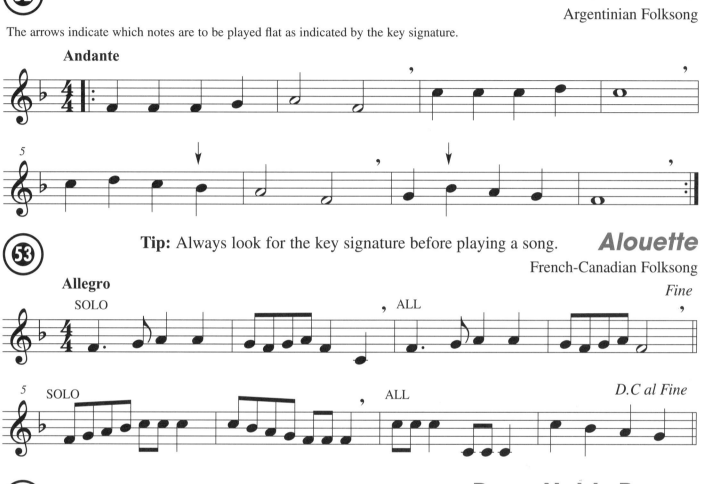

Tip: Always look for the key signature before playing a song.

Alouette
French-Canadian Folksong

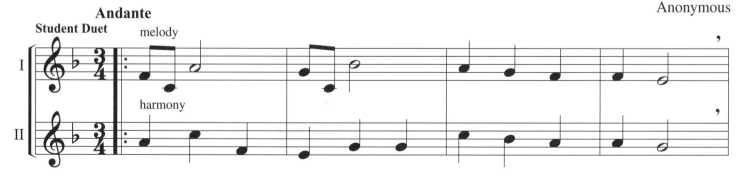

Dona Nobis Pacem
Give Us Peace
Anonymous

 **TIME SIGNATURE**

Music with a $\frac{2}{4}$ **time signature** gets two beats per measure.
Each beat is equal to one quarter note.

Jacob Drink

Polish Folksong

Play several times
with different soloists.

Scotland's Burning

Traditional Round (4 part)

Play several times.

Miss McLeod's Reel

Irish Traditional

Land of the Silver Birch

Canadian Folksong, Round

Play several times.

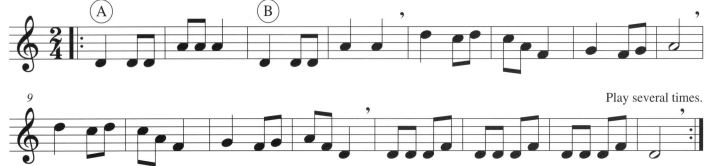

I-1052

KEY OF G

Key of G Warm-up *(Remember all F notes are played sharp (♯)!)*

1

59 **Paw Paw Patch**

American Folksong

Moderato

Student Duet

Switch parts on the repeat.

60 **Simple Gifts**

Joseph Brackett, Jr. (1797–1882)

Moderato

 Use this chart to help you visualize the notes you have learned on the recorder. On a piano keyboard you can clearly see the range of notes that you know and also where the sharps and flats occur.

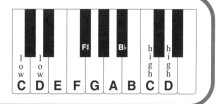

KEY OF C

Key of C Warm-up *(Remember the Key Signature in the Key of C has no sharps or flats!)*

Shortnin' Bread
Southern America Folksong

Morning Has Broken
Gaelic Melody

I-1052

KEY OF F

Key of F Warm-up *(Remember all B notes are played flat (♭)!*

1

🎵 **63**

Down In the Valley
American Folksong

Andante

🎵 **64**

Down by the Station
Traditional Round (4 part)

Allegro

Ⓐ　Ⓑ

Ⓒ　Ⓓ　Play several times.

🎵 **65**

Loch Lomand
Scottish Folksong

Moderato

Bonus Track Don't miss the last track on the Downloadable Recording, *La Volta,* by Michael Praetorius (1571–1621), a respected composer from the Renaissance era (ca. 1450–1600), performed by the **The Jasmin Recorder Consort** on the soprano, alto, tenor, and bass recorders.

GLOSSARY

SIGN	TERM	DEFINITION
	duet	Two different parts of music that can be played together. One part is the melody, the other part is the harmony. (pg. 4)
	embouchure	The way a musician applies the mouth to the mouthpiece of a wind instrument. Pronounced (OMB-a-shur). (pg. 2)
⌢	**fermata**	Indicates that a note or a rest should be held longer than usual. (pg. 13)
	fipple	A fipple is inside the mouthpiece of the recorder. The fipple has a thin channel cut through a solid block. This channel directs the air stream against a sharp edge producing a tone. (pg. 17)
♭	**flat**	Lowers the pitch of a note by a half step. (pg. 26)
	half step	The smallest distance between any two notes. On a piano, a half step is the distance from one key to the very next key, black or white, higher or lower. (pg. 10)
	harmony	Musical tones sounding at the same time. Harmony can also refer to a second part of the music that sounds pleasing with the melody. (pg. 27)
	key signature	The sharps or flats at the beginning of each line of music which indicate the key of the music. The key of C has no sharps or flats in the key signature. (pg. 10)
	legato	Play smoothly. (pg. 5)
	major scale	A series of notes arranged in alphabetical order, ascending or descending. (pg. 23)
	melody	The succession of notes in a song. (pg. 5)
♮	**natural**	Cancels a sharp or flat used earlier. (pg. 18)
	phrase	A succession of notes that make up a musical idea. (pg. 14)
▬ ▬ 𝄽 𝄾	**rests**	Indicate a moment of silence in music. (pg. 4)
	rhythm	The movement of notes in time, sometimes referred to as the timing. (pg. 5)
	round	A song in which the music can be repeated over and over, with the performers starting and ending at different times. (pg. 19)
♯	**sharp**	Raises the pitch of a note by a half step. (pg. 10)
	tempo	Indicates a fast or a slow song. (pg. 5) Three examples of tempo are: *Andante* - a slow, walking tempo *Moderato* - a medium tempo *Allegro* - a fast tempo

I-1052